The insects that run our world

The Helpers and the Pests

Sarah Ridley

WAYLAND
www.waylandbooks.co.uk

First published in Great Britain in 2021
by Wayland

Copyright © Hodder and Stoughton, 2021

All rights reserved

Editor: Sarah Peutrill
Designer: Lisa Peacock
Consultant: Buglife, the Invertebrate Conservation Trust

HB ISBN: 978 1 5263 1405 5
PB ISBN: 978 1 5263 1406 2

Printed and bound in China

MIX
Paper from
responsible sources
FSC
www.fsc.org
FSC® C104740

Wayland, an imprint of
Hachette Children's Group
Part of Hodder and Stoughton
Carmelite House
50 Victoria Embankment
London EC4Y ODZ
An Hachette UK Company

www.hachette.co.uk
www.hachettechildrens.co.uk

Picture credits:
Dreamstime: Marlohagen 8b. iStock: Antagain front
cover tr; Antelopus 8t; Alasdair James front cover tc,15tl;
MediaProduction 4b,7; Riorita 16t; Smuay 9b;Tim UR 12br; Ohne
Titel 16b. Nature Picture Library: Nigel Cattlin 11t,11b,12t,13t;
Premaphotos 15tr; Andy Sands 14t; Nick Upton 18; Visuals
Unlimited 6t. Shutterstock: Agrofruti 20t; Aquariagirl1970
23t; Frank60 front cover br; Frontpage 21; Thijs de Graaf 23b;
Guy42 10b; Ilikestudio 19t; Stewart Innes 13br; D.Kucharski
K.Kucharska 9t; Henrik Larsson 1, 10c, 14b; MattiaATH 19b;
Steve McWilliam 2, 22b; Ruud Morijn Photographer 22t; Pirunpon
17b; AN Protasov 5t; Eddie J Rodriquez 20b; Seregam 5bl; Anna
Seroplani 12bl; Simon Shim 15b; Sofiaworld 17t; Liliya Vantsura
5br; Viktor1 6b; Jen Watson 3, 13bl; Marcin Wolc front cover bl;
Wollertz 4t.

Every attempt has been made to clear copyright.
Should there be any inadvertent omission please apply
to the publisher for rectification.

Elephant hawk moth

Contents

Pests and helpers

People share planet Earth with all the other living things in the natural world, including insects.

Some of these insects make life more difficult for people – they can be pests.

Mountain pine beetles and their young are killing trees in North America.

The vine weevil is one of many insects that like to eat the plants that farmers and gardeners grow for people to eat or enjoy.

Head lice are insect pests that live in our hair.

Some insects can be very helpful to people by eating the insects that are eating crops or garden plants.

This ladybird larva munches the aphids that feed on our plants.

Many insects make things that we find useful, such as honey or dye. Studying insects has also given people ideas that lead to inventions.

Dye made from cochineal bugs

Honey

Can insects make you ill?

Some sorts of fly can make people ill. Mosquitoes can carry malaria and yellow fever in their body liquids and pass them on to people when they bite.

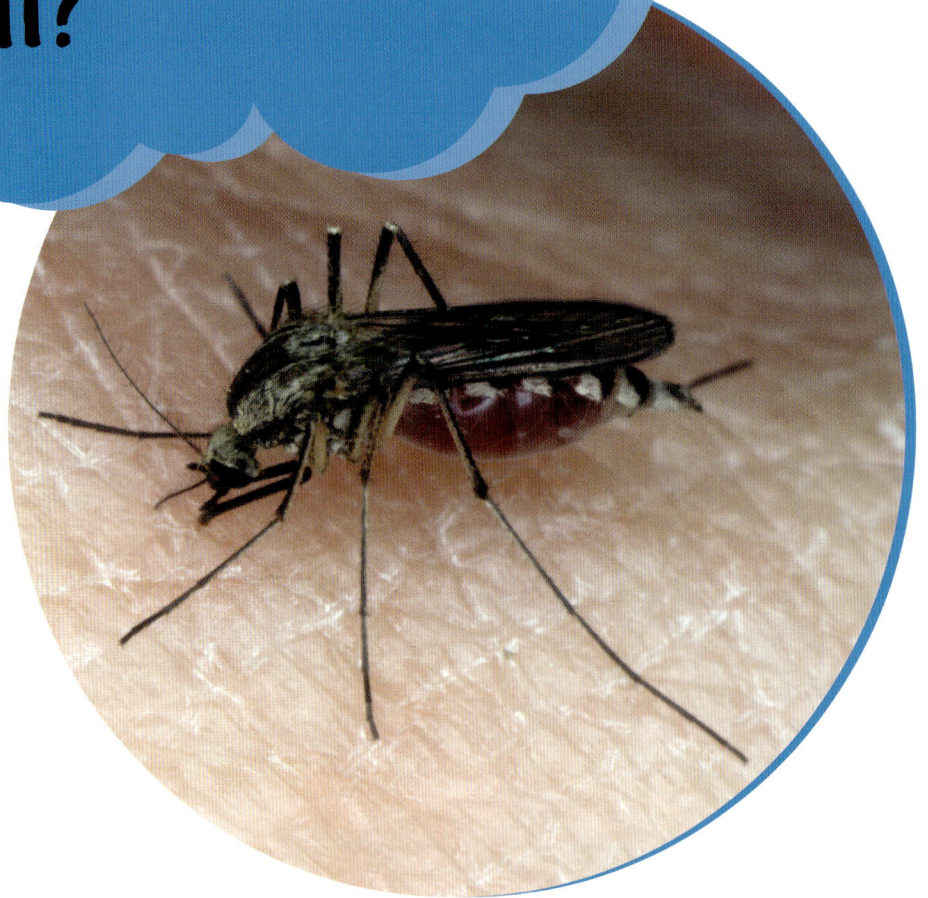

Other insects spread diseases on their feet, all six of them! Houseflies are the main problem as they like to eat poo BUT they also like to eat your food.

The germs on this housefly's feet will stick to the ice cream it is eating.

Cockroaches that live in people's homes mostly come out at night and crawl around, spreading dirt and germs. Ninety-nine per cent of cockroaches live in the wild but if you have them in your home, they are real pests.

Insects also spread diseases in herds of animals kept by people.

Pests at home

Termites

Sometimes insects make your home their home. They can cause a lot of damage.

Some types of termite feed on and live inside dead wood. And sometimes that wood holds your house up!

This beetle baby, or larva, will munch through floorboards, beams or furniture until it turns into an adult beetle.

Woodworm

The caterpillars of clothes moths will eat your carpets, jumpers and blankets. Like all the photos here, it shows the insect much bigger than it is in real life.

Bedbugs hop into luggage, arrive in second-hand furniture or move in from next door. During the day they hide, but at night they creep out to feed on your blood.

Pests in the garden

Visit any garden in summer and you'll see buzzing bees and beautiful butterflies pollinating the flowers. BUT an awful lot of insects eat garden plants.

The lily beetle eats the leaves of lilies and fritillaries.

Aphids

Tiny aphids are bugs that suck sap from plants, making them weak.

These large white butterfly caterpillars will munch and munch on leaves for about four weeks before they turn into pupae.

The young of several types of fly and beetle, including the cabbage root maggot, eat plants' roots.

Cabbage root fly

Earwigs can be pests and helpers as they eat flowers and leaves, as well as aphids and other insect pests.

What's eating my crop?

Farmers around the world look after their crops carefully, watching out for insect pests which can do awful damage. Here are a few of them.

The codling moth's caterpillars burrow into apples and pears.

Codling moth

The chunky leatherjacket eats the roots and shoots of grasses, including wheat, barley and oats.

The Colorado potato beetle and its larvae munch on the leaves of potato plants.

Cotton farmers fear lots of different insect pests, including cotton bollworms.

Grasshoppers and desert locusts eat plants. Every now and then, desert locusts form huge swarms and eat everything in their path.

Desert locusts

Gardeners' friends

This wasp has killed a weevil and will carry it back to its nest.

Wasps can be real pests on a picnic and a wasp sting really hurts. However, for most of its life, a wasp spends its days carrying insect pests back to the nest to feed the wasp larvae.

Other insects are also helpful to farmers and gardeners because they love to eat insect pests.

One ladybird may eat more than 5,000 aphids in its lifetime!

Lacewing adults and larvae eat masses of insect pests.

Adult lacewing

Lacewing larva eating an aphid

Rove beetle

Ants dig tunnels in soil which help plants by bringing air and water to their roots.

Rove beetles run along the ground hunting for grubs, maggots, caterpillars, slugs and aphids to eat.

Marvellous makers

The products insects make for themselves can be very useful to people. Honeybees make honey from plant nectar. They don't make it for us, but as a winter food store for themselves.

Honeybees also make wax to build the honeycombs where they store honey and bring up their babies.

Bees will sting if they get scared, so watch them from a safe distance.

We use beeswax to make candles, make-up, polish and as a waterproof layer to make fruit last longer.

16

Cocoon

Silkworm

Silkworms are the caterpillars of silk moths. When it is time to change into a moth, each silkworm spins itself a silk cocoon.

Long ago people learnt how to unwind the cocoons to make silk thread.

The tiny lac bug of India makes a roof of shellac from a liquid it makes inside its body. Lots of lac bugs live together.

People scrape shellac off branches and use it to make varnish, false teeth and other things.

Shellac

Insect inspiration

Insects have given people some really good ideas.

Paper wasps make nests from chewed wood and spit. Three hundred years ago this inspired a scientist to ask why people didn't make paper out of wood too. After a while, people worked out how to do it.

A cockroach can squeeze into tiny spaces and survive people treading on it.

The body of a cockroach has inspired scientists to create a robotic cockroach to use in disaster areas after an earthquake or explosion.

Insects help people solve crimes. Special detectives study the flies, eggs and maggots on a dead body to work out how long ago someone died. They know how long it takes for insects to find a dead body and start their life cycles.

Scientists are trying to find out how mealworms and wax moth caterpillars can eat plastic. It could lead to a solution for getting rid of plastic waste.

Mealworms

19

Insects in trouble

This farm worker is spraying pesticide over fruit trees to kill insect pests but this can kill or harm helpful insects too.

Some insects are helpful to people and others are not, but they are all connected to other living things. Today, insects are in trouble as there are far fewer of them than there were fifty years ago.

In many places there are huge fields with no hedgerows or beetle banks where insects can live.

In other places, people cut down forests and woods to make way for homes or farming. The insects that lived in this part of the Amazon rainforest died out or left.

Scientists think that climate change will increase the number of insect pests as shorter, warmer winters will give them more chance to have young.

Ways to help

There are ways we can all help insects.

This farmer has planted a strip of wildflowers to support insects and other wildlife. You could grow wildflowers in a plant pot.

Ask your parents or carers to leave an area of your garden wild, mow the lawn less and grow plants along fences and walls. This will give insects more places to live.

An elephant hawk moth feeds on honeysuckle.

If you grow herbs such as mint, oregano and sage next to plants that aphids and other pests enjoy, the strong smell may confuse the insect pests.

Ask your parents or carers if they can buy organic foods, grown without the use of pesticides. Try growing your own organic food.

Organic tomato plant

Be curious. Find out about insects so that you can learn how to support them. Join Buglife, the charity that helps insects and minibeasts and look out for insects wherever you go.

Green shield bug

Glossary

beetle bank A grassy mound dividing a large field to provide homes for insects that eat insect pests.

bug An insect with sucking mouthparts.

climate change A change in the normal weather around the world.

cocoon A case of silk threads that some insects make to protect themselves while they change from larvae into adults.

crop Plants grown by farmers for food.

dye A substance used to change the colour of something.

germ A small living thing, usually a virus or bacterium, that causes infections or diseases.

grub Another name for a beetle larva.

larva Insect young.

leatherjacket The young of a crane fly (daddy-long-legs).

life cycle The different stages of life of a living thing.

maggot The young of a fly.

malaria A serious disease that causes fever and shivering.

mealworm The larva of a darkling beetle.

nectar A sweet liquid made by plants.

pesticide A chemical liquid or powder used to kill harmful insects or weeds.

pollinate The act of moving pollen between flowering plants to fertilise the egg cells.

pupa Part of the life cycle of many insects between larva and adult stages.

sap The liquid inside a plant.

swarm A large group of insects moving together.

yellow fever A deadly disease that is spread by mosquitoes. The disease makes some people's skin turn yellow.

Index

24